IRVING HARPER WORKS IN PAPER

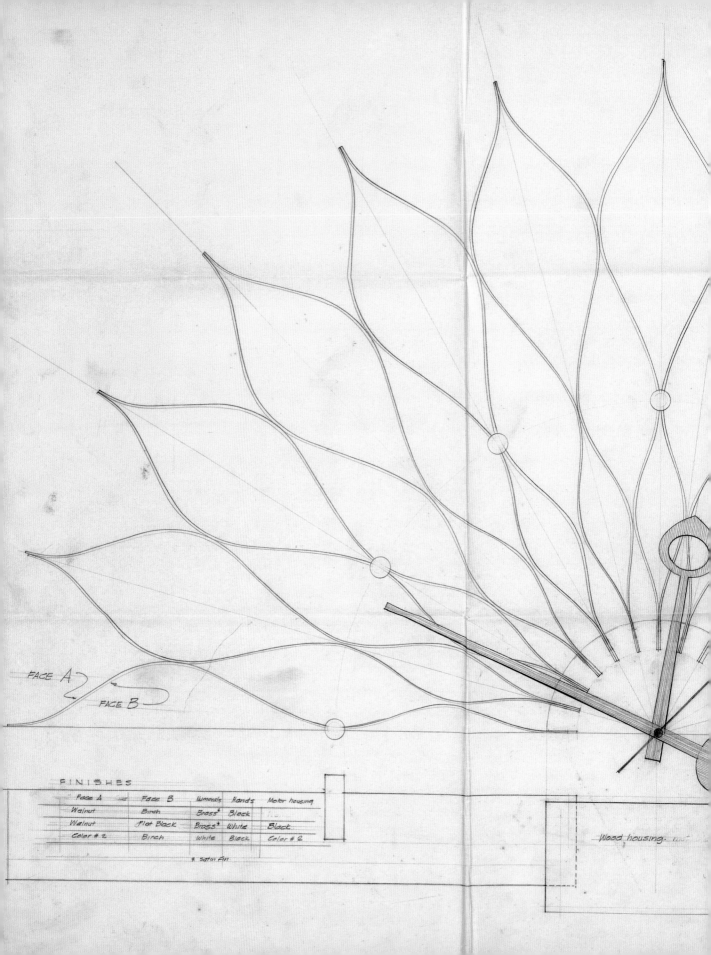

FACE A

FACE B

	Face A	Face B	Numerals	Hands	Motor housing
	Walnut	Birch	Brass*	Black	n.a.
	Walnut	Flat Black	Brass*	White	Black
	Color #2	Birch	White	Black	Color #2
			* satin fin		

Wood housing: n...

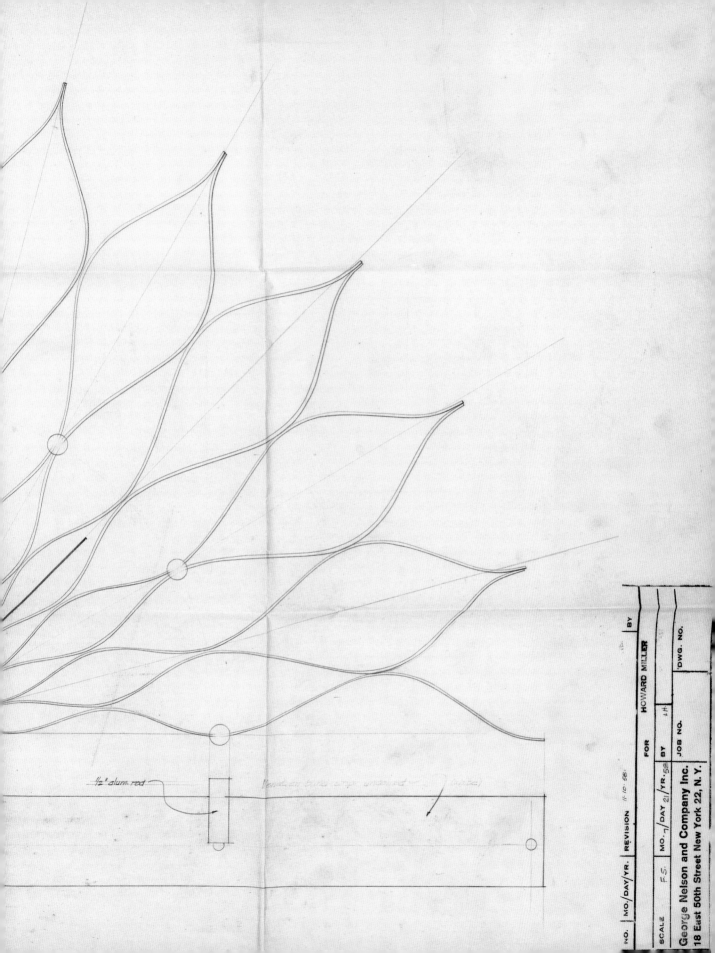

½" alum. rod

NO. | MO./DAY/YR. | REVISION 11·10·58·

SCALE F.S. MO. 7/DAY 21/YR·58 BY LH

FOR HOWARD MILLER BY

JOB NO. DWG. NO.

George Nelson and Company Inc.
18 East 50th Street New York 22, N. Y.

IRVING HARPER WORKS IN PAPER

EDITED BY MICHAEL MAHARAM

CONTENTS

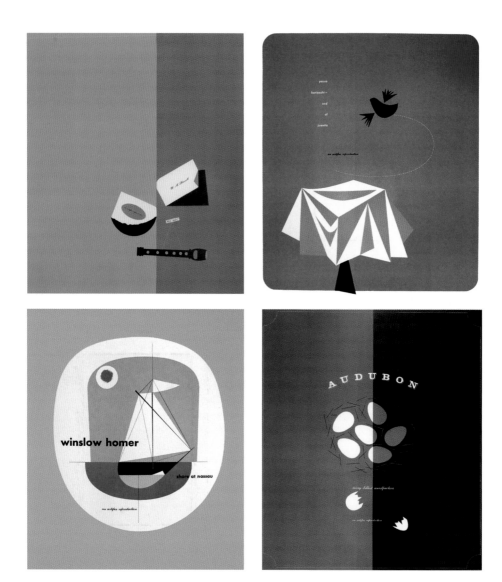

Pages 2–3: Howard Miller Sunflower Clock, technical drawing, 1958
Page 4: Irving Harper portrait by Leslie Williamson, 2011
Page 6: Contact sheet of Irving Harper portraits, early 1950s
Page 8: Artifax sales folders, 1949, 20×17.5 inches

FOREWORD
MICHAEL MAHARAM

It was once the case that design and the people who executed it were largely anonymous. In the second half of the nineteenth century, this began to change. The studios of William Morris and Christopher Dresser, the Wiener Werkstätte, and the Bauhaus all turned out brilliant work that moved design forward, but those who found acclaim tended to be charismatic, conceptual forces who brought new ideas to public light—creators, yes, but also influential editors of a refined sensibility, directing over the shoulders of designers who labored at their instruction. By the 1950s, marketing had become a popular tactic, and celebrity a widespread factor in the persona of products. George Nelson stood tall in this crowd—a bright and worldly New York archetype with a good eye and a gift for banter, whose work cut across the fields of interior, industrial, and exhibition design.

In the 1940s, Nelson began a long association with Herman Miller, and subsequently, the clock manufacturer Howard Miller. As a furniture designer and design director at Herman Miller, he recruited such innovators as Charles and Ray Eames, Alexander Girard, and Isamu Noguchi. The Nelson office also continued to work independently on its own designs, contributing to the invention of many familiar elements of modern living, including the shopping mall, the multi-media presentation, and the open-plan office system. The man who stood behind Nelson through his most pivotal years and iconic products was Irving Harper, whose accomplishments have only recently come to receive the attention they merit.

Our very personal experience with Irving Harper began in 2001 with the re-edition of textile designs he had created for George Nelson fifty years earlier. We had come upon samples of these obscure textiles, and, with thanks to former longtime Herman Miller and George Nelson employee Hilda Longinotti, subsequently learned of Irving, who had spent seventeen years with Nelson and was responsible for much of the Nelson studio's best-known work, including the Marshmallow Sofa, countless Howard Miller clocks, and the enduring 1950s-era Herman Miller logo.

Irving lives near Manhattan, so I phoned him up spontaneously and was greeted by a lively eighty-four-year-old who was eager to assist. Through our collaboration, he shared his sense of having been overshadowed by Nelson and overlooked by design history. Though he never thought to try a computer, as thanks, I purchased an iMac for him in hopes of igniting his curiosity. Together we made his first trip to Google, where I typed in his name and watched his awe at the record of his accomplishments—an incredibly touching moment.

During my visits with Irving, I couldn't help but be amused by the amazing menagerie of paper sculptures he had created over forty years, and which kept him company as he spent nearly every day reading in his glass-enclosed sun porch. A decade passed, and I made a long overdue visit and found Irving to be as sturdy as ever at ninety-five. His collection hadn't fared as well under the sun, dust, and neglect, and I proposed that we restore and document these fragile works to create a lasting record, and perhaps share them with a broad audience. We're pleased to do so here, with the cooperation of Herman Miller and Vitra, and hope you find the lesser-known side of the little-known Irving Harper to be as charming and expressive as we do.

Left:
Howard Miller Ball
Clock, 1949

Right:
Herman Miller Marshmallow
Sofa, 1956–65
(reissued in 2000)

Left, right, and bottom:
Chrysler Pavilion at
the World's Fair, New York,
1964

IRVING HARPER'S WORLD

JULIE LASKY

In 1963, Irving Harper, director of design at George Nelson Associates and author of several of the twentieth century's most evocative household artifacts, including the atom-like Ball Clock (1949) and festive Marshmallow Sofa (1956), was a nervous wreck. He had been put in charge of the team designing the Chrysler pavilion for the 1964 New York World's Fair, and he was coping with an ambitious program, a tight schedule, and high expectations.

Four years before, the Nelson office had worked on a monumental exhibition in Moscow for the United States Information Agency. That show, of which Nelson was creative director, included a jungle gym filled with American consumer products and a model home in which Nixon and Khrushchev wrestled for cultural supremacy in their infamous "Kitchen Debate." Harper's contributions were minimal; he took care of the rest of Nelson's clients while much of the office, which had expanded to meet the demand, poured its energies into demonstrating the wonders of capitalism. Now, once again, Nelson had been recruited to promote American industrial power, and this time on American turf—the very place in Queens where the 1939 World's Fair had ushered in modernity.

Harper disliked the giant stainless-steel globe in Flushing Meadows Park that occupied the place where the Trylon and Perisphere, symbols of the '39 Fair, once stood. He had been one of five signatories of a telegram sent jointly to President John Kennedy and New York Governor Nelson Rockefeller in 1961 that complained that the distinctly unmodern symbol, known as the Unisphere, "is probably one of the most uninspired designs we have ever seen," one that threatened to "reflect seriously against United States prestige."[1]

Located between Ford and General Motors, the Chrysler pavilion was anything but banal. Harper's design required that the site be flooded and divided into islands linked by bridges. Each island represented a different facet of car making—design, engineering, production—and had a singular feature: a gigantic walk-in engine with pistons shaped like monster heads that pumped up and down and sent off showers of sparks; a garden of auto parts; a rocket signifying Chrysler's contributions to the space program. Visitors were guided by automatic chair through the entire production sequence. Almost fifty years later, Harper recalled the pavilion as a "wonderful project." But he conceded that it almost drove him to knit.[2]

1. Ira Henry Freeman, "3 Nations to Shun 1964 Fair in City," *New York Times*, February 18, 1961.

2. Irving Harper, interview with the author. Unless otherwise indicated, all direct quotes from Harper derive from conversations conducted on August 16, 2010; September 7, 2010; February 14, 2011; March 21, 2012; and June 16, 2012.

Irving Harper in his home
attic studio, Rye, New York

Left and right:
Sculptures in paper
and wood window-blind
matchsticks

Harper was looking for an activity to take his mind off the stress—something repetitive and soothing he could do at home in the evening. He considered taking up knitting or crocheting, but he also excelled at building cardboard models for client presentations. One day, he split apart a bamboo window blind and used Duco Cement to reconstitute the matchstick-size pieces into a flowing mask, which he set on a carved wood pedestal.

For the next four decades, Harper made sculptures. He built them mostly out of paperboard, but also balsa wood, beads, straws, toothpicks, pinecones, telephone wire, twigs, dolls' limbs and glass eyeballs, Mylar sheets, Styrofoam lumps, and pieces of the ceramic clocks he designed for the Michigan-based company Howard Miller. He scouted Manhattan art galleries and the Metropolitan Museum of Art for inspiration and fashioned Egyptian cats and stylized antelope heads, Byzantine towers, African masks, a Renaissance Florentine church in relief. He built constructions stacked like molecules, and abstractions that peeled off the picture plane like a grid of flames. He worked in the styles of Surrealism and de Stijl and made study after study of Picasso, the artist he admired above all others. On his shelves, Guernica's suffering humans and horses mingled with crows, antelopes, and throned Egyptian animal gods.

Nineteen sixty-three, his year of *agita*, was also the year in which Harper left the Nelson office, where he had been working since 1947, and went out on his own. He disliked the hustle of running his own business and soon formed a partnership with a fellow Nelson alumnus, Philip George, designing primarily interiors for such clients as Braniff International Airways and Hallmark Cards. When Harper retired, in 1983, his sculpture output stepped up. By the time he had built his last work, around 2000—a glass-eyed owl sheathed in brown paperboard feathers—the collection approached some three hundred pieces. Harper stopped making art, he insists, because he ran out of room to display it in the old farmhouse in Rye, New York, where he had been living for half a century.

Harper still lives in that house, surrounded by those pieces, in a *gesamtkunstwerk* of which he, at ninety-six, is not only the creator but also a central, vital component. Individually, the sculptures can be appreciated for their charming translations of art historical masterpieces, their structural ingenuity, or their deft expressions of color. They are arresting down to the hinge, piercing, or loop. Collectively, they form a sumptuous catalogue of one man's perambulations along the boulevards of twentieth-century aesthetics. Arranged in simple, bright rooms among primitive artworks and contemporary furniture—much of which are Harper's own prototypes—they testify to the playfulness and omnivorous cultural appetites of the era's great modernist designers. No less than the Eames House, the Harper interior is eclectic. Permeated with a calm sense of artistic adventure, it reflects lives joyfully lived.

And lives imaginatively created. Harper is not the designer's original name. He was born Irving Hoffzimer on July 14, 1916, in New York City. The oldest child and only son in a family of three children, Irving spent his early years in a tenement building at 288 East Fourth Street, on the Lower East Side. His father, David, had emigrated from Austria; his mother, Rebecca, from Poland. They spoke Polish and Yiddish.[3]

3. According to Ellis Island documents, Harper's father, David, was born in Krakan, Austria, and arrived in New York on November 15, 1907, on the *Pretoria*, sailing out of Hamburg, Germany. He was twenty-three years old, illiterate, and had ten dollars in his pocket. The family name on the ship's manifest is spelled Hofzimmer. Later, in the U.S. Census of both 1920 and 1930, it appeared as Hoffzimer.

Howard Miller plastic
birdhouses, 1954–55

Opposite:
Molded vinyl lanterns
(distributed by Richards
Morgenthau), 1962

Net Lights, 1959

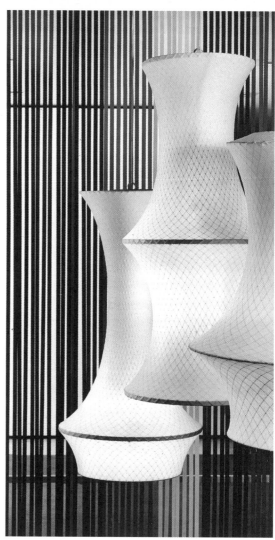

Howard Miller Lastex
table and wall lamps, 1952

Left:
General Lighting scissor
arm wall light, 1947–48

Right:
Koch and Lowy Half Nelson
table lamp, 1949–50

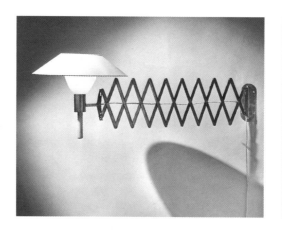

David Hoffzimer was a bookbinder who specialized in novelty books that recorded a baby's important early moments: first smile, first tooth. His workshop was across the street from the family home, and Irving spent hours there playing with paper and cardboard. (Decades later, his daughter, Elizabeth, who was born in 1953, occupied herself similarly as a child, making paper cutouts on the floor of Harper's third-floor home studio in Rye, while he worked at his desk.) Later, the Hoffzimer family moved to Brooklyn's Borough Park neighborhood, and Irving attended New Utrecht High School. After graduating, he enrolled at both Brooklyn College, where he pursued a liberal arts education, and the Cooper Union for the Advancement of Science and Art, where he took classes in architecture three nights a week. Out of his daylight studies bloomed his avocations: a lifelong appreciation of art, literature, and classical music. (Elizabeth recalls, "Once, in very small elevator, he recognized Stravinsky. He was paralyzed. He didn't know what to say.")[4] The evenings bred his vocation: the design and construction of objects.

4. Elizabeth Harper Williams, interview with the author, March 16, 2012. All subsequent citations derive from this conversation.

It wasn't a smooth career beginning. "In those days architecture was completely flat—there were no jobs," Harper recalls. He "went the round of architecture offices" and was hired by Morris B. Sanders, who lived and worked in a pioneering modernist building he had erected at 219 East 49th Street. The United States was still recovering from the Great Depression, and Harper recalls that the project that kept architects alive at the time was the 1939–40 New York World's Fair. Sanders, an Arkansas native, had been commissioned to build the fair's Arkansas pavilion, and Harper was assigned to work on the interior displays.

"So I had to give up the idea of becoming an architect and instead became a designer," he recalls. It was a happy fortuity. Harper found design "much more interesting because it was entrepreneurial." In an architecture office, it's "hard to rise to the top," he points out. And "design work is more varied. Everything is a first-time thing. You learn a lot more."

Harper soon left Sanders to work for Gilbert Rohde, the advertising illustrator-turned-product designer, who was instrumental in introducing modern design to America through his furniture for Herman Miller and Heywood-Wakefield. Harper worked as a draftsman for Rohde and "did occasional furniture design," he says. While waiting to be interviewed, he met another job candidate, a designer who had recently emigrated from Germany named Ernest Farmer. The two men became colleagues at Rohde's office and close friends. "He was a wonderful character," Harper recalls today of Farmer. "Very gentle, very warm...the prototype of everybody's lovable uncle."

Around that time, Harper adopted his name. The imperative to shed his identity was as urgent as the one that caused him to jettison his architectural career plans. It came, however, at the behest of his wife-to-be, Belle Seligman, a lawyer who lived in his Brooklyn neighborhood and whom he had met through participation in left-wing political activities. Irving and Belle were both members of the American League against War and Fascism, an organization founded in 1933 by communists and socialists who were alarmed at the rising fascist threat in Europe. "We used to meet regularly at her house and other places. We got to know each other that way," Harper says. They were married when Irving was twenty-four and Belle twenty-three.

Left:
Herman Miller
advertisement for the
Marshmallow Sofa, 1956

Opposite:
Advertisement for
Herman Miller, late 1940s

Left:
Herman Miller product
brochures (designed by
Irving Harper with Don
Ervin, Dick Schiffer, and
Tony Zamora), 1960

Advertisements for
Herman Miller, late 1940s

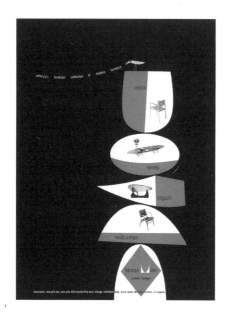

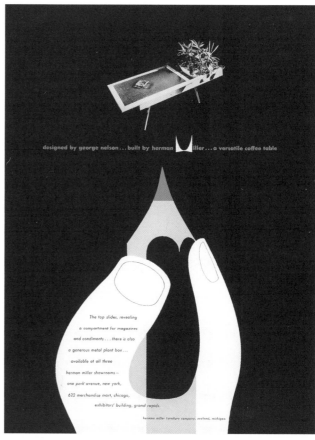

herman **iller furniture features exclusively designed hardware.** *

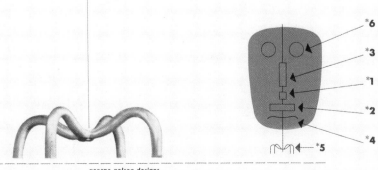

george nelson designs

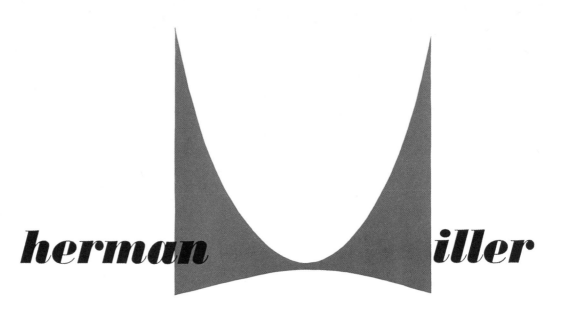

Before Belle would agree to marry him, however, she insisted that he change his surname. "She refused to be named Hoffzimer," Irving says. "She suggested Harper, and I said okay. And I regretted it. I'm not a Harper. Harper is too bland, too American. It doesn't have much character." One could argue that Hoffzimer, a variation of the German word for a courtyard room, wonderfully evokes a man who has accomplished much in the sheltered nooks of more flamboyant personalities, but who also, judging from the popularity of his designs, has persistently trained his vision on the central action. Yet Harper had other reasons to detach himself from his origins. His mother, resentful when he announced his plan to move out of the family home, cut ties. "She made me heavy with guilt that I made that decision," Harper says now. "It took me a long time to get over it. I had two sisters; I didn't see them for years. I see my younger sister [Phyllis] now, and I haven't seen my middle sister [Sophie] for seventy-two years." He adds that Belle's parents, Benjamin and Minnie Seligman, "were totally different types. They were easy to get along with, understanding. They had happy lives. So there was this general air of contentment about her place that I soaked up."

When the United States entered World War II, Gilbert Rohde cut back his design practice, and Harper joined the Army Corps of Engineers, moving to Norfolk, Virginia, but only briefly. He was given the routine draftsman's job of making sketches of airfields and airplanes. "I got fed up with it," he says. He enlisted in the navy as an ensign, becoming a communications officer (Lieutenant, Junior Grade) on the U.S.S. *Woodworth*, a destroyer in the Pacific. Harper calls his navy tenure "a pleasant experience…I used to take phone messages and communicate them to the captain on the bridge. I was reamed out because I used to decode them improperly, but I survived." He experienced only one night of combat: while on anti-mining duty, his ship brought down a Japanese plane that was searching for bigger cruisers and battleships.

Rohde suffered a heart attack in a Manhattan restaurant and died in 1944 at the age of fifty. When Harper demobilized the next year, he joined the office of Raymond Loewy, where he designed department store interiors. He was "totally bored," he relates. "Loewy had a shop divided into three parts: design office, detailing office, estimating office. It was like a production line. I was glad to get out of there."

Relief came in 1947, in the guise of Ernest Farmer. Harper's associate from Rohde's office was now a member of the design company founded two years before by the architect and journalist George Nelson. According to Harper, Farmer persuaded Nelson to hire him to design graphics, thus launching a long, productive chapter in Harper's career.

The chapter began with his logo for Herman Miller, a modified version of which is still in use. After Rohde's death, Nelson became the furniture company's first director of design, and according to his biographer, Stanley Abercrombie, Nelson wanted the graphic artist Paul Rand to create the logo and ads for a new campaign. Herman Miller's founder, D. J. DePree, suggested that the Nelson office take a crack at the campaign instead.[5] Harper rendered an ad featuring a big *M* on a wood-grain-patterned background that evoked the wood furniture that would be part of the new collection. The pieces were still in production, and Harper had to design the ad in a vacuum. "They had no photos of furniture," he recounts, "nothing to go by…I did [the *M*] with a French curve. The top was done with one

5. Stanley Abercrombie, *George Nelson: The Design of Modern Design* (Cambridge, MA: MIT Press, 2000).

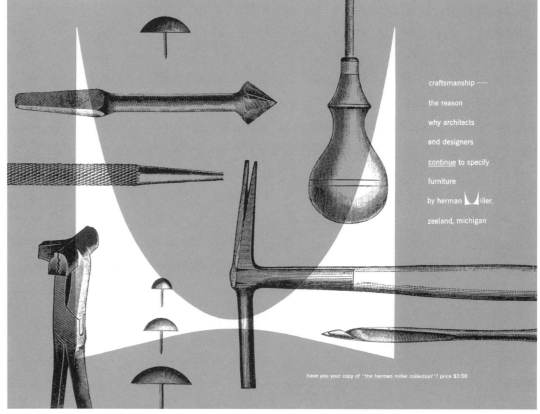

the herman miller e*xecutive* o*ffice* g*roup*

Left:
Howard Miller clocks,
1949–ca. 1963 (reissued
by Vitra since 1999)

Right:
top and bottom:
Howard Miller clock
prototypes in
foamcore and wood

Irving Harper in his
Jane Street apartment,
New York City, 1945

part of the French curve, the bottom with another part. Two straight lines, and that was it."

Another project for Nelson that led to durable fame was Harper's clock designs for Howard Miller, a company spawned by Herman Miller and named after D. J. DePree's brother-in-law, who led it. "They kept coming out of me; I never went dry," Harper says about the scores of ebullient starburst- and elliptical-shaped wall and desk clocks that have become shorthand for mid-century modernism and its revival in contemporary design.

But Harper is still rankled by Nelson's account of the Ball Clock's origins. It's a wonderful story of how Nelson was entertaining his friends Isamu Noguchi and R. Buckminster Fuller over drinks one evening, and the men, along with Harper, began sketching ideas for clocks. Nelson claimed he found a drawing of the Ball Clock among the pile the next morning and was uncertain who had produced it but suspected Noguchi. The truth is much less colorful, Harper insists: "I was given the job to design clocks," he says, "so I just designed it. There was no routine collaboration." Harper's efforts to correct the historical record have been futile, he despairs, because Nelson's version, which can be heard in the impresario's own voice in an audio file on Herman Miller's website,[6] "seems to have more life to it."

"George didn't give me much credit," Harper says. "I was allowed to sign the ads for Herman Miller. That was pretty much all." The question of authorship at the Nelson office has been a prickly subject for years. "George Nelson was a very intelligent man, an articulate speaker, and a top-notch writer, but not a designer," Harper says. "He didn't sit down at a drafting board." Among the designers in Nelson's stable who created the memorable products for which he is known were John Pile (Pretzel Chair), Charles Pollock (Swag Leg Armchair, developed under Pile's supervision), George Mulhauser (Coconut Chair), and Ronald Beckman and John Svezia (both worked on the Sling Chair with Harper). Only lately has attention been beamed on these talented subordinates, though it remains widely acknowledged that Nelson was a brilliant instigator and editor of their work.

Far from bitter, Harper speaks about his time with Nelson affectionately. Referring to the office, he recently told the illustrator Matte Stephens, "It looked disorganized and hard to control but it let people express themselves and some pretty good stuff came out of it."[7] Hilda Longinotti, Nelson's receptionist and muse for twenty years, described her boss as "the orchestrator, the idea giver. He made suggestions, he doodled—that was his favorite expression. And he never interfered with Irving." She recalls Harper in those days as a "quiet, self-effacing man" who "always dressed like Columbo," the slovenly TV detective played by Peter Falk in the '70s. "Everyone else in the office had a uniform and they all emulated George. They wore gray trousers with a little buckle in the back—George had bought his in a British shop—and red suspenders. But Irving never paid any attention to this. He always wore sneakers. George carried an aluminum attaché case that was very novel back then. Not Irving. I don't think he had an attaché case."[8]

Longinotti also noted a playful current under Harper's recessive demeanor that accounted for the joviality of many of his designs. ("Both Ernest and I were fanatical Bauhaus fans and we tried to fit everything into that mold," Harper recently told Herman Miller's editorial director, Sam Grawe. "Later on I got a little bit more

6. "George Nelson: The Ball Clock," audio file, "Discovering Design: George Harold Nelson," Hermanmiller.com, accessed April 5, 2012, http://www2.hermanmiller.com/discoveringdesign/#topic=3.

7. Irving Harper, interview with Matte Stephens, "Irving Harper," *Design Sponge*, October 11, 2007, accessed April 22, 2012, http://www.designsponge.com/2008/03/a-special-podcast-matte-stephens-and-irving-harper.html.

8. Hilda Longinotti, interview with the author, March 27, 2012.

Howard Miller clocks,
1949–ca. 1963 (reissued
by Vitra since 1999)

Visitor Information Center,
Colonial Williamsburg,
Virginia, 1955–58

Opposite:
New York Times
Information Center,
New York City, 1954

United States Travel
Services (USTS),
multiple locations, 1962

Opposite left:
Herman Miller Showroom,
Chicago

Opposite right:
The first Herman Miller
catalog, 1948

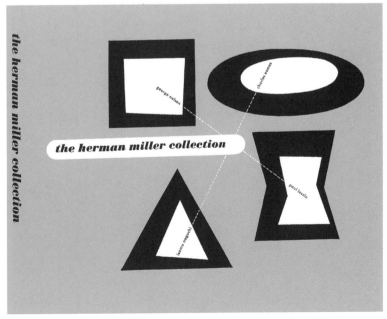

Left:
Schiffer Pavement fabric
pattern, 1950 (reissued
by Maharam in 2002)

Right:
Schiffer China Shop fabric
pattern, 1950 (reissued
by Maharam in 2002)

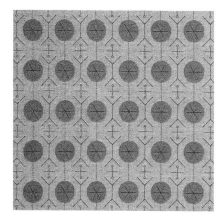

Bloomingdale's architectural
competition winning entry,
1947

Left to right:
Fine-tip Sharpie drawing
by Irving Harper.

American beech tree
on the Harper property,
Rye, New York.

"Harper" sign attached
to the barn.

flexible. I betrayed the Bauhaus.")[9] Once, when Nelson was departing on one of his frequent trips to Europe, Longinotti related, Harper rounded up the entire office and followed Nelson to Idlewild (now JFK) airport to wish him bon voyage. As Nelson crossed the tarmac, the staff unfurled a brown-paper sign from the observation deck. Far from amused, Nelson took money out of their salaries to pay for the billable hours they wasted.

And though Harper did not receive recognition for his remarkable array of projects—from textiles (his Pavement and China Shop fabrics designed in the early 1950s for Schiffer Prints were revived by Maharam in 2002) to a portable slide projector for Airequipt to the cultish Marshmallow Sofa for Herman Miller, which began as an experiment in working with machine-made upholstered cushions (the technology was a failure, and the cushions had to produced by hand)—his name did get out. A 1947 *New York Times* article announced his victory in an architectural competition sponsored by Bloomingdale's. Harper took first prize for his design of a four-bedroom contemporary house with a flat roof and wood siding, even though Nelson is credited with the furniture that was in the imagined house's model living room exhibited at the department store: "a two-piece coffee table of primavera birch" and a "pair of lacquered chests... typical examples of Nelson storage pieces."[10] (Or more likely, typical examples of Ernest Farmer storage pieces.)

The publicity was not always happy. In 1966, the *New York Times* reported that Harper had lost an envelope filled with photos and plans for the Museum of Modern Art exhibition *The New City: Architecture and Urban Renewal*. Harper was the show's freelance designer and had left the envelope on the commuter train he took home to Rye.[11] "Oh, my God, he was really absentminded," his daughter, Elizabeth, remembers today. "He got off the train and drove home and when he got home he realized he didn't have the plans and was all panicked. I think they found them in Stamford." Before the envelope was recovered two days later, Harper broke the bad news to Arthur Drexler, then director of MoMA's architecture department. Though the episode ended well, Harper believes it destroyed their friendship.

In 1960, the *Times* published Harper's home in Rye with the headline: "Modern Furnishings Adapt Roomy Old House to Young Family's Living."[12] Irving and Belle had bought the three-story shingled farmhouse, built in 1895, after outgrowing their small apartment on Jane Street in Greenwich Village. They moved there in 1954, when Elizabeth was one. The Harpers looked in Westchester County, north of Manhattan, because it was on the way to their weekend home in Pawling, New York, and chose the house on Brevoort Lane because it stood on nearly an acre of land, in the shelter of a magnificent beech tree. (Today, Harper's drawing of the tree is propped up in his front hall—the only artwork displayed among his large, colorful collection that offers a clue to his drafting skills.)

"I came here and saw this place and said, 'This is where I'm going to die,'" he says. He tore down a wall of the sun porch to enlarge and brighten the living room. Beneath the expanse of windows, he built a long wooden shelf wrapping around two sides of the room. "I had to do something with it," he says of the shelf. "I put plants there at first"—a row of pots with long, leafy fingers is visible in the *Times* article—"but the plant shelf became smaller and the art became bigger."

9. Irving Harper, interview with Sam Grawe, March 2, 2012. All subsequent citations derive from that conversation.

10. Mary Roche, "Exhibit Will Open for Home Planner: Architectural Models, Interiors and New Furniture Shown at Bloomingdale's," *New York Times*, February 7, 1947.

11. "Modern Museum Loses Plans for Exhibition," *New York Times*, December 23, 1966.

12. "Modern Furnishings Adapt Roomy Old House to Young Family's Living," *New York Times*, May 30, 1960.

China Service for
Walker China, 1952–53

Opposite:
Carvel Hall Leisure
stainless-steel cutlery,
1955–56

Melamine Service Florence
for the Prophylactic Brush
Company, 1952–55

Opposite:
Fraser's cutlery prototype
and technical drawing,
1950s

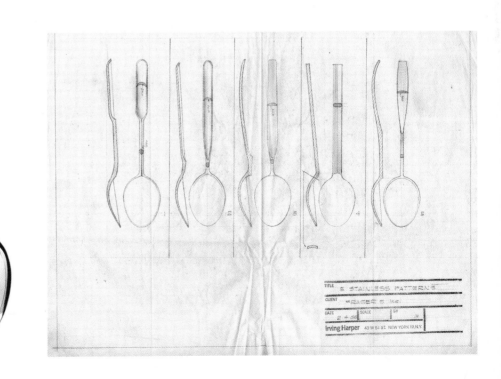

Sculpture with muffin tin
and doll parts

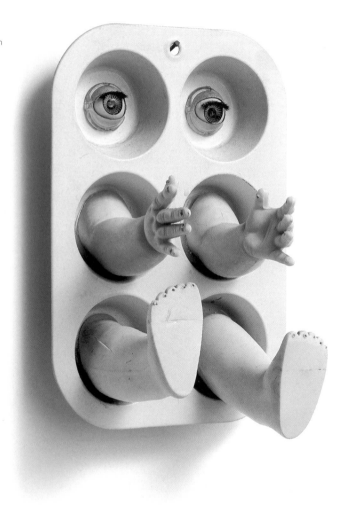

Today, that shelf is a place of honor for Harper's sculptures. It holds his first and last creations—the mask from 1963 and the owl from the turn of the millennium—along with an angel in a cloud of toothpicks and tiny pinecones, a cluster of Picasso-esque figures, a rhinoceros with Mylar armor, and antiquities and art pieces produced by other hands. Works carefully placed throughout the rest of the house—as well as those that became damaged through the effects of time on fragile paper and were retired to the barn at the back of Harper's property—reveal his waves of interest. A series of masks with sharply angled features tip viewers off to his passion for African art. "I saw things at the Metropolitan Museum's African collection and thought I'd love to have one for myself, but I knew it would be out of my reach," he explains. Wall pieces with fields of lavender, green, and gold paper dots tacked to the picture surface have the shimmering effect of Impressionist paintings. Balsa wood sculptures range from desktop models to large, delicate scaffolds flagged with colored paper and preserved in Plexiglas boxes. Animals and birds interested him because of their variety of shapes—"One thing you don't have with human beings," he says.

Elizabeth notes that Harper's Surrealist phase began when she was "a kid and growing out of my dolls and putting them aside. Originally, he would use arms and legs and heads and do stuff with them, but then he liked the eyes. Eventually he ran out of the eyes of my dolls and he started buying them wholesale. I used to carry them around with me."

"I'd be on a roll with a certain kind of design," Harper says. "I'd have a sort of rough mental picture of what I wanted to do." New ideas came from working out structural problems or from seeing a concept at an exhibition that could be translated to paper. "I would get ideas from the gallery but I wouldn't make drawings. I'd just get started." He only regretted not being able to install outdoor sculptures on his roomy property. One attempt, a large bird built with exterior-grade plywood that he hung from a tree, disintegrated, he insists, "partially because I didn't build it properly. I was a lousy craftsman."

Harper rarely showed the sculptures outside of his home. They appeared in a group exhibition in SoHo, at a solo show upstate in Rochester, and in an event staged in his barn. When a sculpture broke while on loan in nearby New Rochelle, he spurned every subsequent request to exhibit the works. Friends considered it the highest honor when he agreed to part with one as a gift, a gesture he indulged in only after years of steady production. A woman who saw the SoHo show was interested in buying a piece; Elizabeth communicated the message to Harper, who had declined to attend the opening. How much would he charge? Elizabeth asked. "How much would a Modigliani sell for?" Harper returned. (Suffice it to say, more than the potential buyer was willing to spend.)

"I never sold any of my pieces," Harper says today. "I had all the money I wanted. Then I would have lost my sculptures and just had more money. I just wanted to have them around."

Belle died on December 22, 2009, after sixty-nine years of marriage. Today, Harper lives alone in his art-filled house. The third-floor studio looks untouched from the days when he meticulously assembled his sculptures, not because he was a patient man, acquaintances say, but because he was mesmerized by

Airequipt portable
slide projector and paper
prototype

Opposite:
Howard Miller fireplace
accessories, 1951

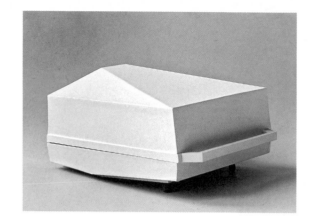

Herman Miller Thin Edge
Bed, 1954

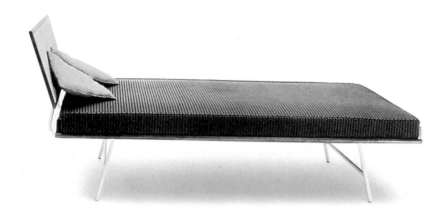

Irving Harper with
Howard Miller fireplace
accessories, 1951

Irving Harper in his living room, Rye, New York

Irving Harper in his living room, Rye, New York, 2009

a ritualistic craft that also required imaginative problem solving. A reproduction of *Guernica* is tacked to a slanting wall, near a composition by Harper that has similar elements—contorted positions, Cubist perspective, a dynamic mass of figures and abstractions. A photo of a young Elizabeth playing the violin is posted above a picture of Irving in his late thirties or early forties. He has thick, dark eyebrows and a crewneck shirt and looks somewhat strained and bemused and more like George H. W. Bush than Columbo.

"It's amazing that I don't have the slightest desire to do them anymore," he says in his light-flooded living room, where he spends most of his time reading, listening to music, and appreciating his handwork. He recently recalled for Sam Grawe the days before he had turned the room into a modernist tableau. "I remember I had a circular saw in the living room, and I was building this counter around the room, and I was living here for the time being. I didn't have any things on my own to decorate it with and hadn't bought any accessories. So George [Nelson] came by and he looked at all these blank spaces and this blank counter and said, 'There's nothing here.' I don't know if he meant that as a form of flattery. I rather doubt it. Too bad he can't come by and take a look at it now."

PREVIOUS PAGE:
WOOD WINDOW-BLIND MATCHSTICKS, FOUND WOODEN STAND
6.25 X 11.5 X 7 INCHES

THIS PAGE:
PAINTED CONSTRUCTION PAPER, PAPERBOARD
7 X 10 X 15 INCHES

WOOD WINDOW-BLIND MATCHSTICKS, FOUND WOODEN STAND
6.25 X 11.5 X 7 INCHES

TOOTHPICKS, STRING, CHAINS OF STAINLESS-STEEL BEADS, COSTUME JEWELRY, FOUND HAT FORM
10 X 18.5 X 11 INCHES

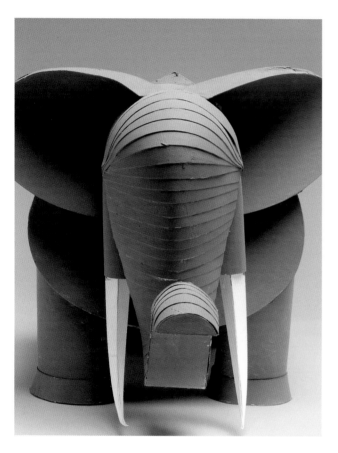

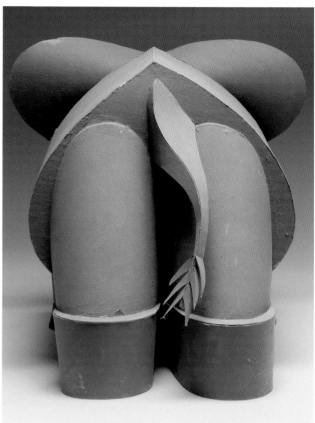

PAINTED PAPERBOARD, CONSTRUCTION PAPER
18 X 10 X 9 INCHES

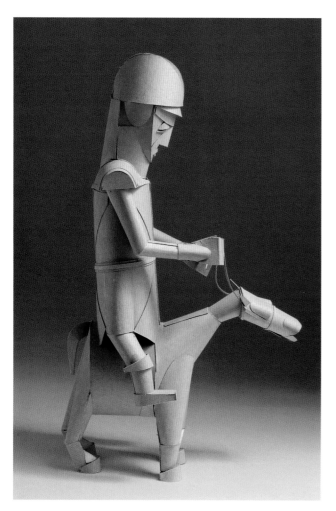
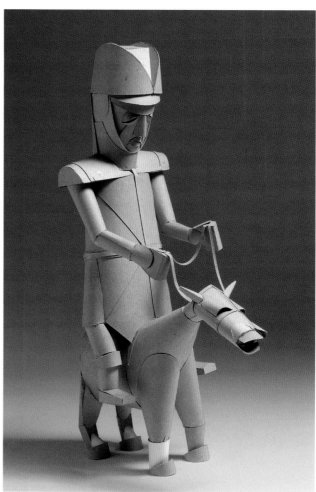

PAPERBOARD
6 X 10.5 X 18.5 INCHES

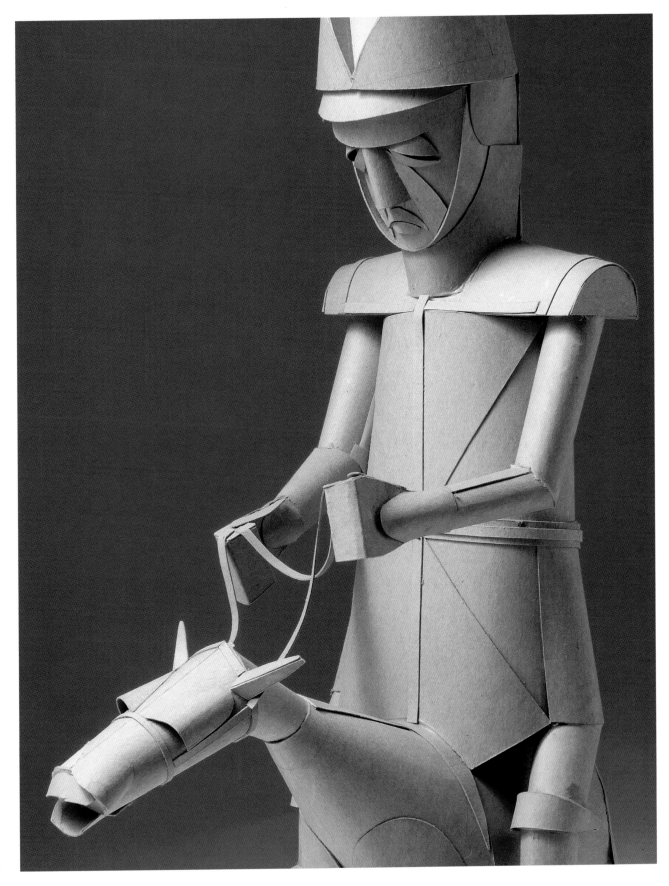

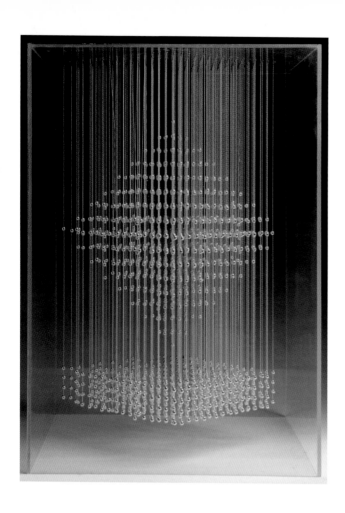

CHAINS OF STAINLESS-STEEL BEADS (MODEL OF A HYATT REGENCY FOYER, KANSAS CITY)
10.25 X 14.5 X 10.5 INCHES

CONSTRUCTION PAPER, PING-PONG BALL
7X13.5X17.75 INCHES

WOOD WINDOW-BLIND MATCHSTICKS, PAINTED CONSTRUCTION PAPER, COTTON THREAD
20X22X25 INCHES

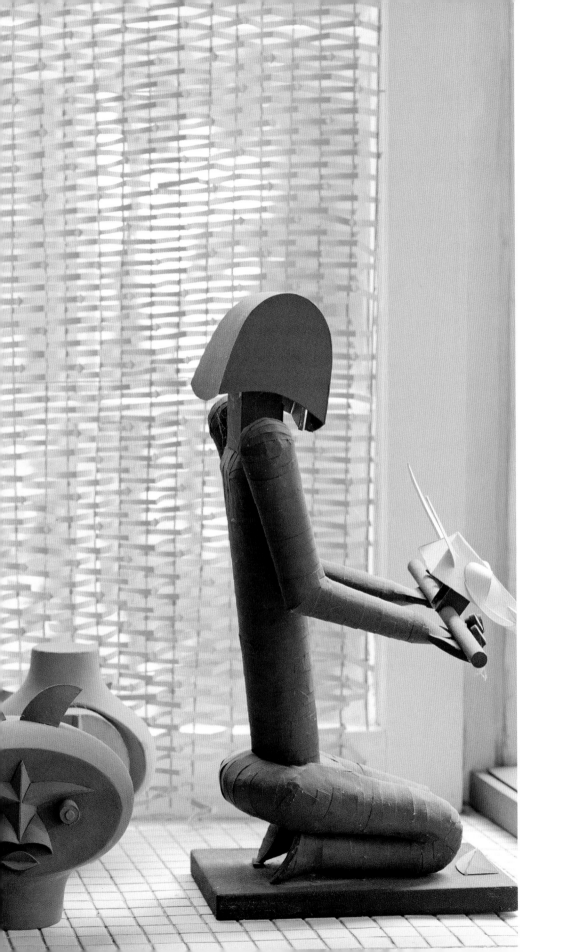

PAINTED PAPERBOARD
10X10X16 INCHES

LEFT TO RIGHT:
PAINTED CERAMIC CLOCK HOUSING PROTOTYPES, PAINTED CONSTRUCTION PAPER
7X4.5X7, 7X6X7, 6X4X7.5, 9X9.5X5.5 INCHES

PAINTED PAPERBOARD, FOUND BIRD'S NEST
5.5X5.5X16 INCHES

OPPOSITE:
TOOTHPICKS, NYLON STRING, PINECONES, STORE-BOUGHT BALSA-WOOD FIGURE
14X22X14 INCHES

CONSTRUCTION PAPER, WOOD BASE
28X12X9 INCHES

PAINTED PAPERBOARD, MAT-BOARD, WOOD BASE
19X27X13 INCHES

PAPERBOARD, TOOTHPICKS, CLOCK PARTS, PEARLS, PLASTIC EYES, WOOD BASE
19X13.5X9.25 INCHES

COLOR CONSTRUCTION PAPER, FOUND HAT FORM
14X8X19 INCHES

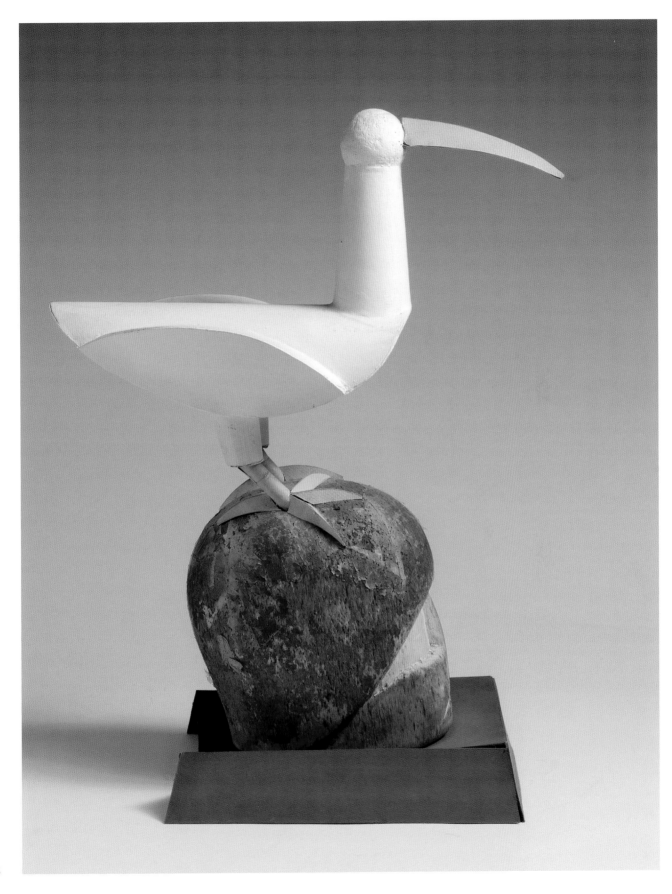

LEFT TO RIGHT:
HOLE-PUNCHED, PAINTED CONSTRUCTION PAPER
7X6X25 INCHES

PAINTED CONSTRUCTION PAPER
11X10X26.5 INCHES

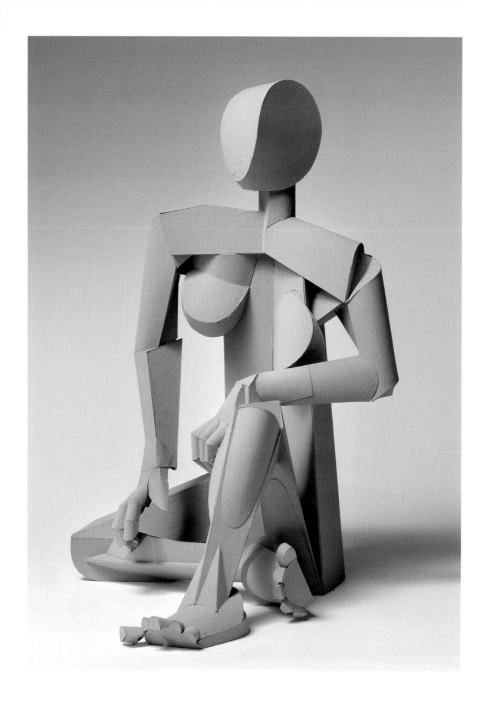

CONSTRUCTION PAPER
12X19X19 INCHES

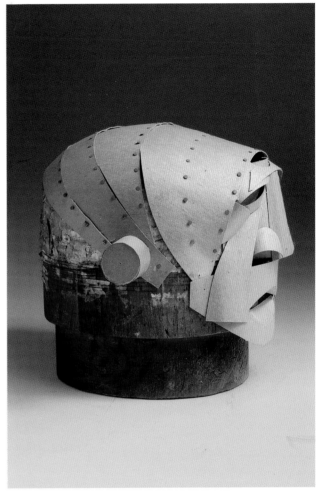

CHIPBOARD, NAILS, FOUND HAT FORM
9X8X8.5 INCHES

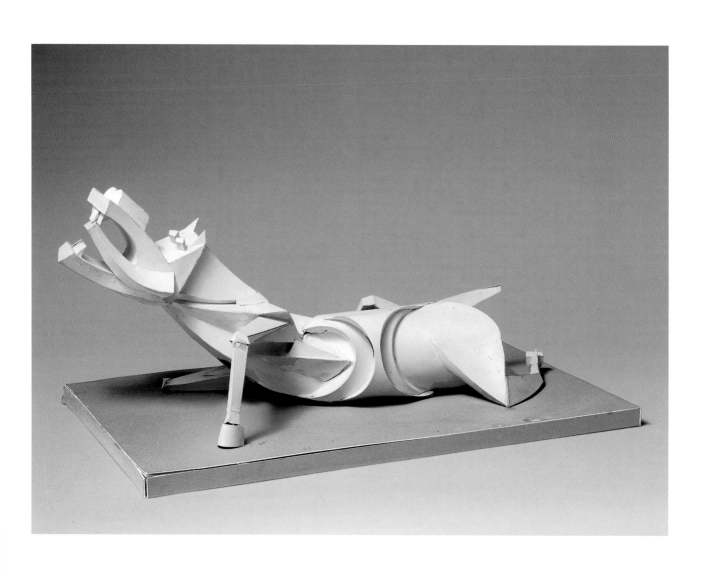

PAINTED PAPERBOARD
23X13X10 INCHES

PAINTED PAPERBOARD
18X3X10 INCHES

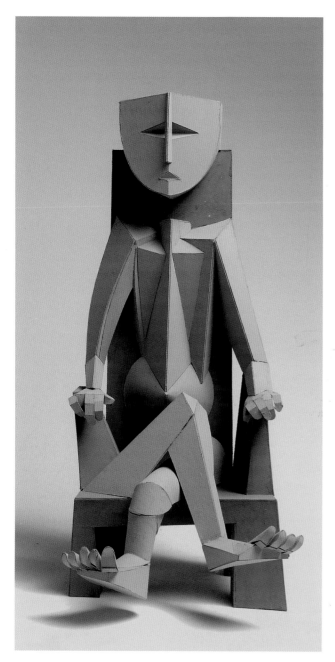

LEFT TO RIGHT:
PAINTED PAPERBOARD
7X8X18.5 INCHES

PAPERBOARD, WOOD BASE
10X9.5X18 INCHES

OPPOSITE:
PAINTED CONSTRUCTION PAPER, FOUND WOODEN SPINDLES, WOOD BASE
8X19.5X9.5 INCHES

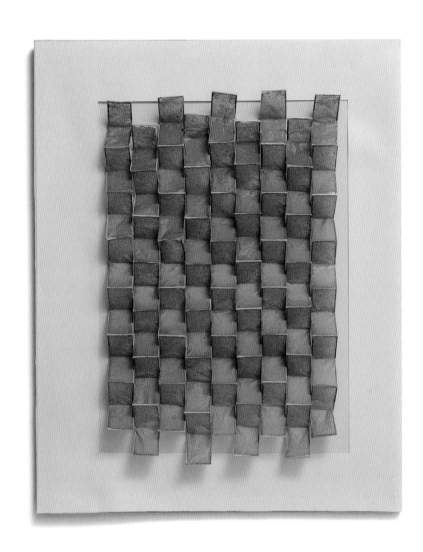

MAT-BOARD, BALSA WOOD, JAPANESE TISSUE PAPER, WOOD BASE
16X25X2 INCHES

CONSTRUCTION PAPER, TWIG, WOOD BASE
7.5 X 26 X 7.5 INCHES

WOOD WINDOW-BLIND MATCHSTICKS, BALSA WOOD,
COLOR CONSTRUCTION PAPER
18 X 26.5 X 10 INCHES

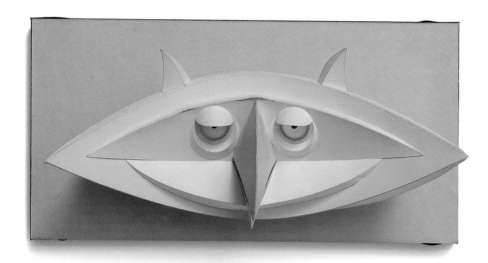

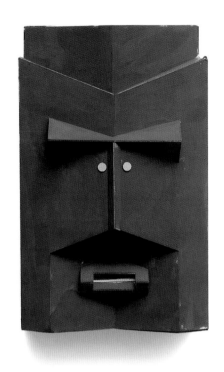

PREVIOUS SPREAD, TOP LEFT TO BOTTOM RIGHT:
PAINTED VACUUM-FORMED PLASTIC PACKAGING, GLASS DOLL EYES
6X8.5X3 INCHES

PAPERBOARD
18X9X7.5 INCHES

PAINTED CONSTRUCTION PAPER
6X9X4 INCHES

PAPERBOARD
10X12X4.5 INCHES

CONSTRUCTION PAPER, PING-PONG BALLS, WOOD STAND
5X21.5X5 INCHES

PAINTED PAPERBOARD, WOOD DOWEL
9X16X5 INCHES

PAINTED CORRUGATED CARDBOARD, PAINTED PING-PONG BALLS, TWIGS,
PAPERBOARD BASE
14X16.5X5 INCHES

PAINTED PAPERBOARD
6.5X10.5X4 INCHES

THIS PAGE
CONSTRUCTION PAPER, MIRROR, PAINTED PING-PONG BALLS, PAPERBOARD BASE
26X29X15 INCHES

PAINTED PAPERBOARD, MANILA PAPER, WOOD FRAME
32.75X39.75X4 INCHES

LEFT TO RIGHT:
PAINTED CONSTRUCTION PAPER
12X17.75X4.5 INCHES

PAPER, WOOD WINDOW-BLIND MATCHSTICKS, METALLIC MYLAR, BEADS
9X14X9.5 INCHES

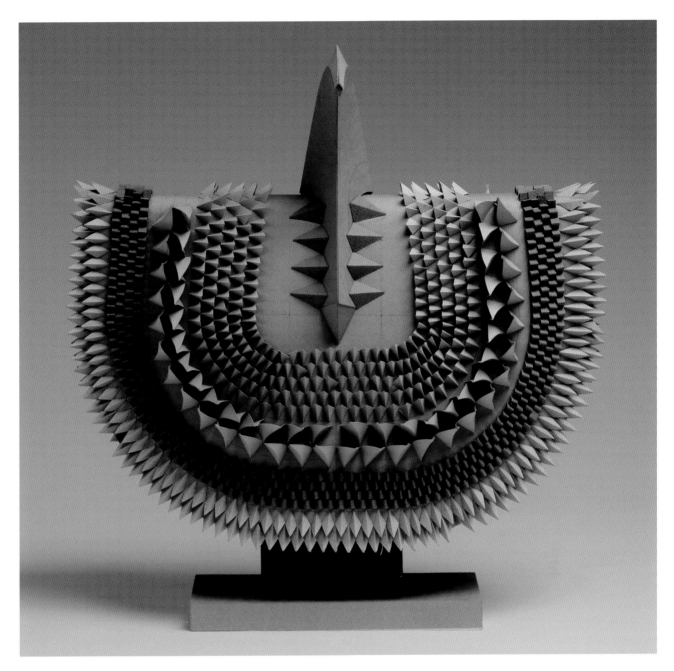

PAPERBOARD, CONSTRUCTION PAPER BASE
15.75 X 16.75 X 7.5 INCHES

LEFT TO RIGHT:
CONSTRUCTION PAPER
16.25 X 57 X 16.25 INCHES

CONSTRUCTION PAPER, MAT-BOARD, FOUND WOOD SPINDLES
7 X 19 INCHES, 7 X 30 INCHES

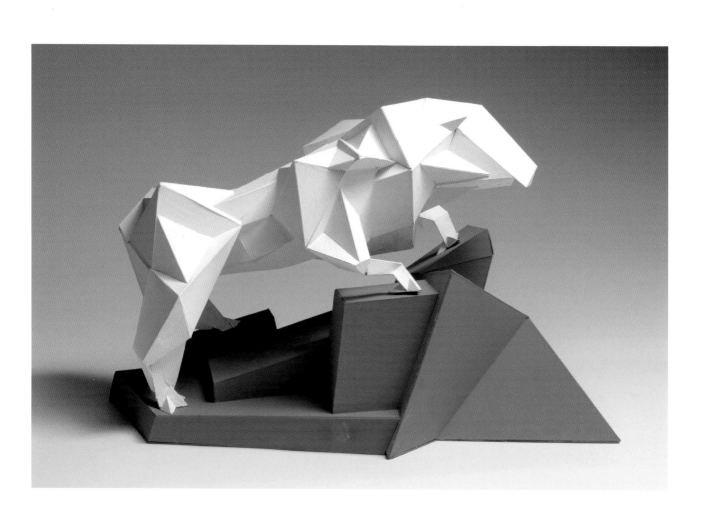

PAINTED PAPERBOARD
18 X 11 X 12.5 INCHES

PAINTED PAPERBOARD
14 X 16 X 12 INCHES

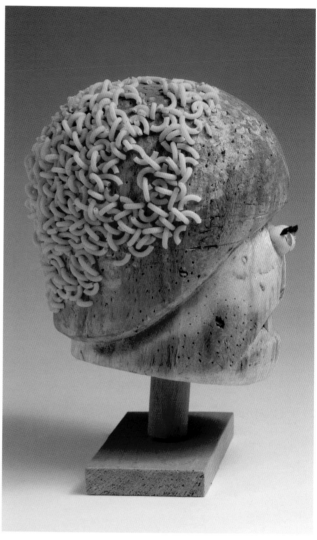

DRY PASTA, GLASS DOLL EYES, WOOD, FOUND HAT FORM
8X6X10 INCHES

OPPOSITE:
PAPERBOARD
12X12X37 INCHES

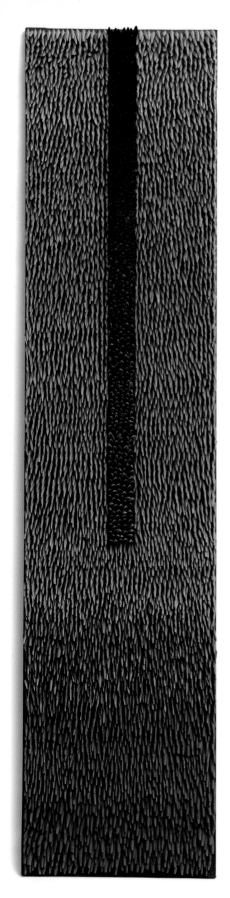

COLOR CONSTRUCTION PAPER, PAPERBOARD, WOOD BASE
15X63.5X3 INCHES

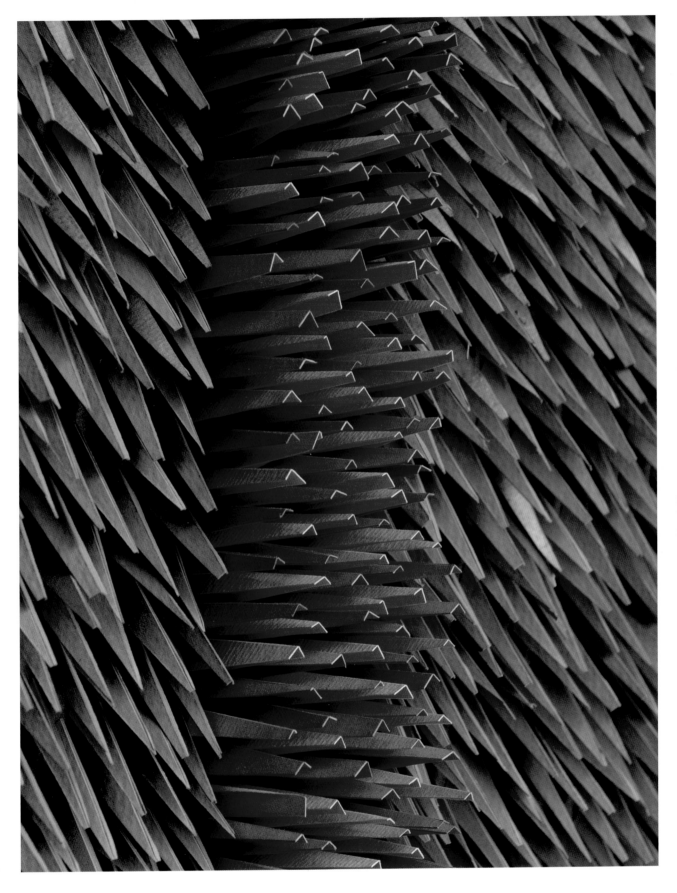

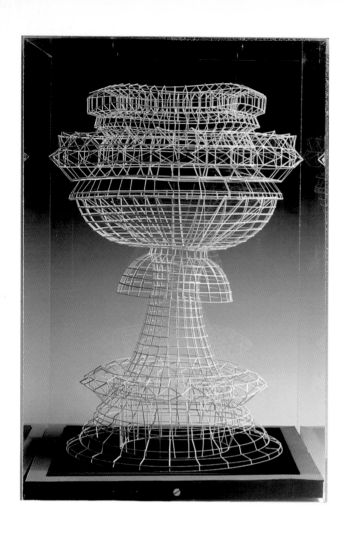

WOOD WINDOW-BLIND MATCHSTICKS, MAT-BOARD, CLEAR FISHING LINE, WOOD BASE
13X13X19 INCHES

LEFT TO RIGHT:
BEADS, SHELLS, GLASS DOLL EYES
6X6X10 INCHES

CONSTRUCTION PAPER, TREE BARK
7X12X8 INCHES

CONSTRUCTION PAPER, MOP HEAD
8X16X7 INCHES

CLOCK PARTS, GLASS DOLL EYES
14X14X12 INCHES

LEFT TO RIGHT:
CONSTRUCTION PAPER, BRANCHES
7X12X9 INCHES

CONSTRUCTION PAPER, BRANCHES
9X5X14 INCHES

WOOD CHIPS, FOUND HAT FORM
7X14X9 INCHES

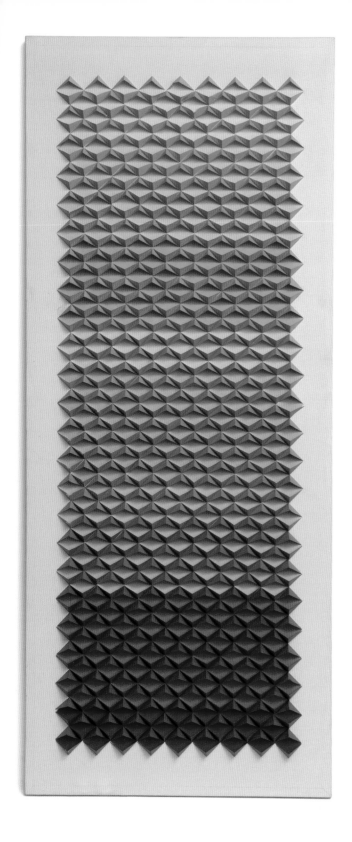

COLOR CONSTRUCTION PAPER, WOOD BASE
24 X 57 X 1.5 INCHES

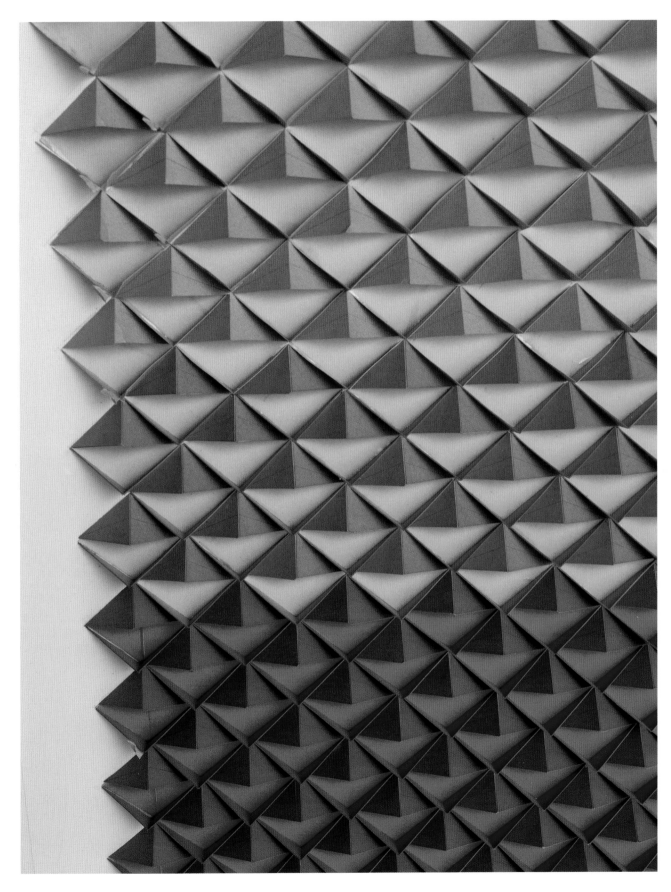

MAT-BOARD, FOUND CYLINDER WOOD BASE
7X6X14 INCHES

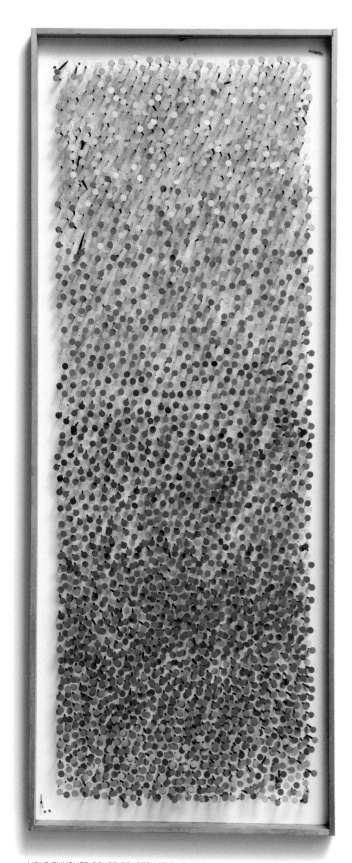

HOLE-PUNCHED COLOR CONSTRUCTION PAPER, MAT-BOARD, TOOTHPICKS, WOOD FRAME
12X30X1.5 INCHES

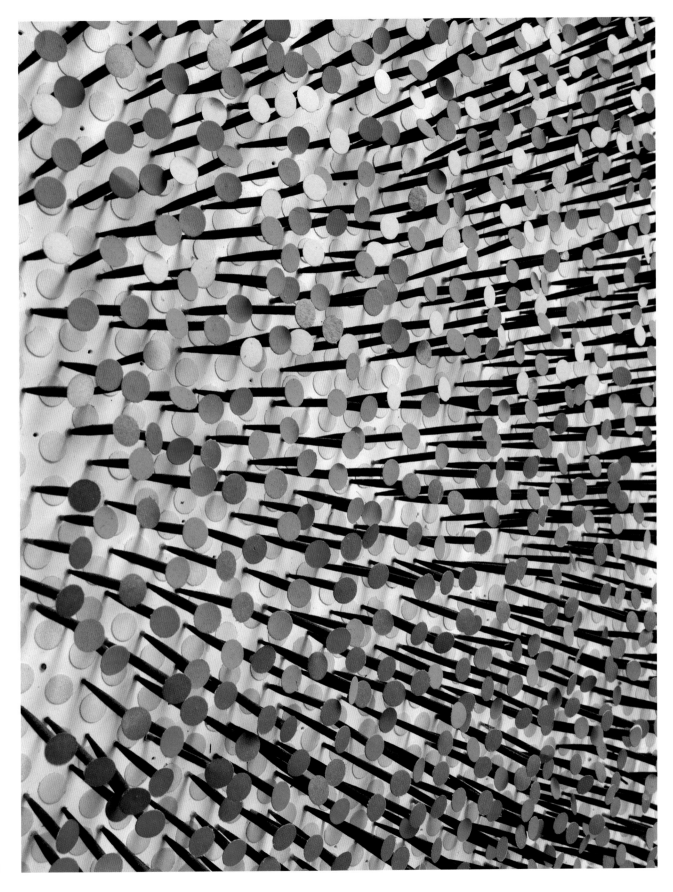

CONSTRUCTION PAPER
8X12X9 INCHES

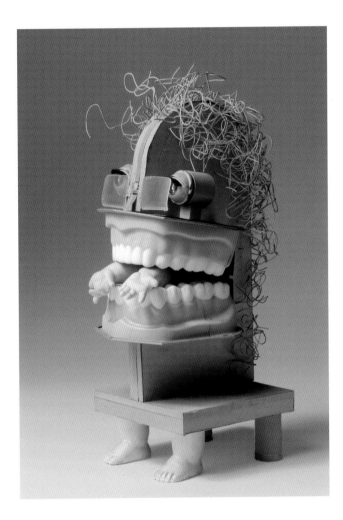

LEFT TO RIGHT:
PLASTIC TEETH, TELEPHONE CABLE WIRE, DOLL EYES, HANDS, AND FEET
6X14.5X7 INCHES

PAPERBOARD, WOOD, STAINLESS-STEEL BEADS, MAT-BOARD BASE
8X8X9 INCHES

HOLE-PUNCHED COLOR CONSTRUCTION PAPER, TELEPHONE CABLE WIRE, MAT-BOARD, WOOD FRAME
18.5X30X2 INCHES

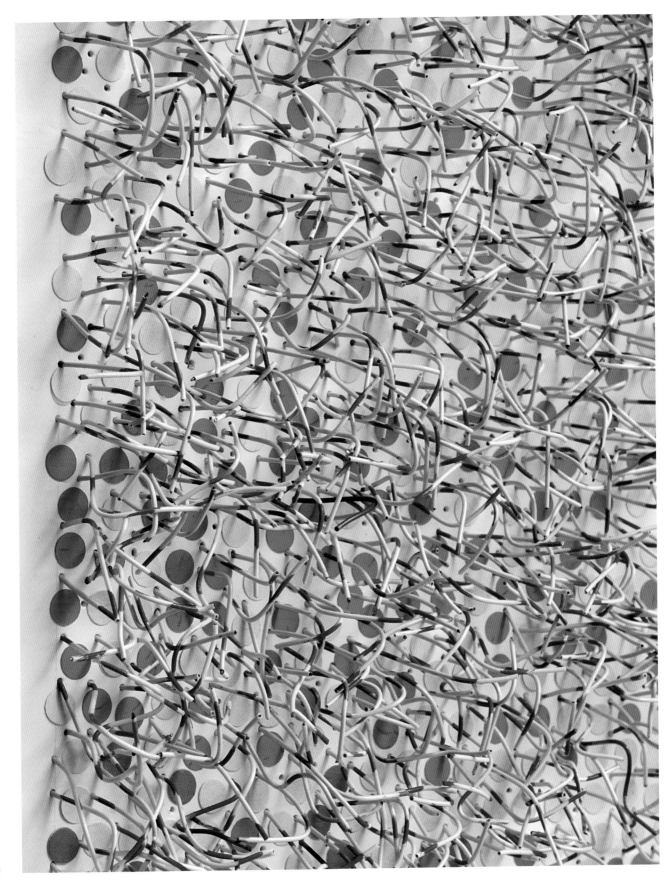

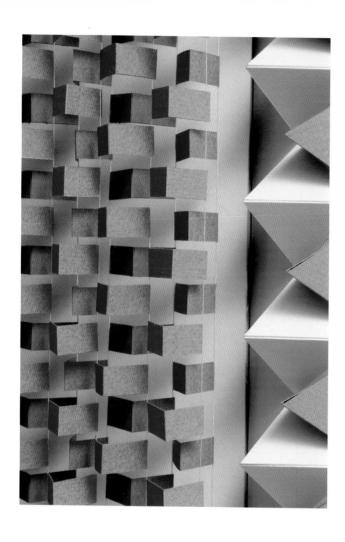

COLOR CONSTRUCTION PAPER, COTTON THREAD, WOOD FRAME
21X31X4.5 INCHES

CONSTRUCTION BOARD, TELEPHONE CABLE WIRE, WOOD BASE
20.5 X 28.5 X 3.5 INCHES

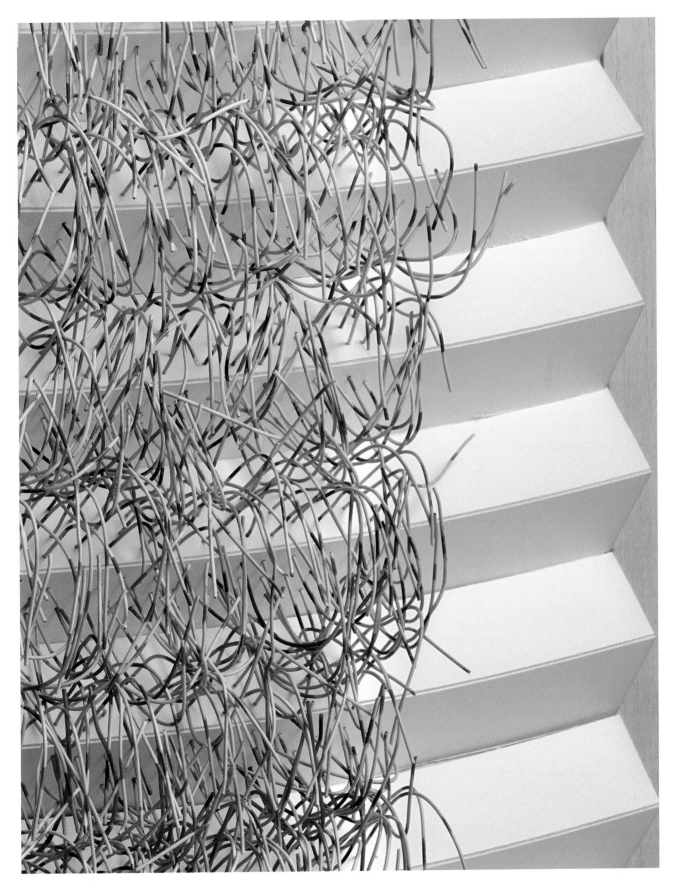

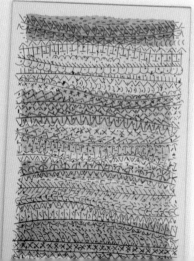
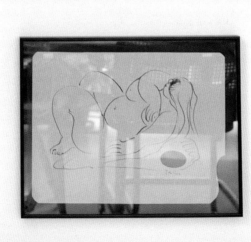

COLOR CONSTRUCTION PAPER, MAT-BOARD, WOOD FRAME
14.75 X 9.25 X 1.75 INCHES

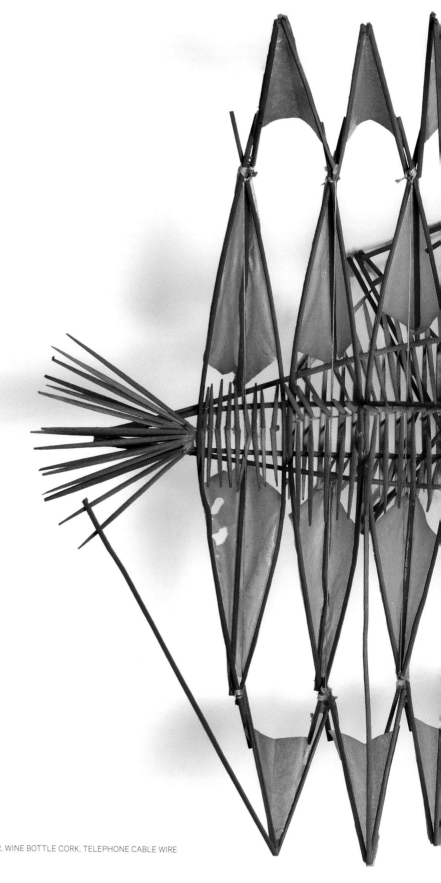

PAINTED WOOD STICKS, TOOTHPICKS, JAPANESE TISSUE PAPER, WINE BOTTLE CORK, TELEPHONE CABLE WIRE
14 X 18 X 7 INCHES

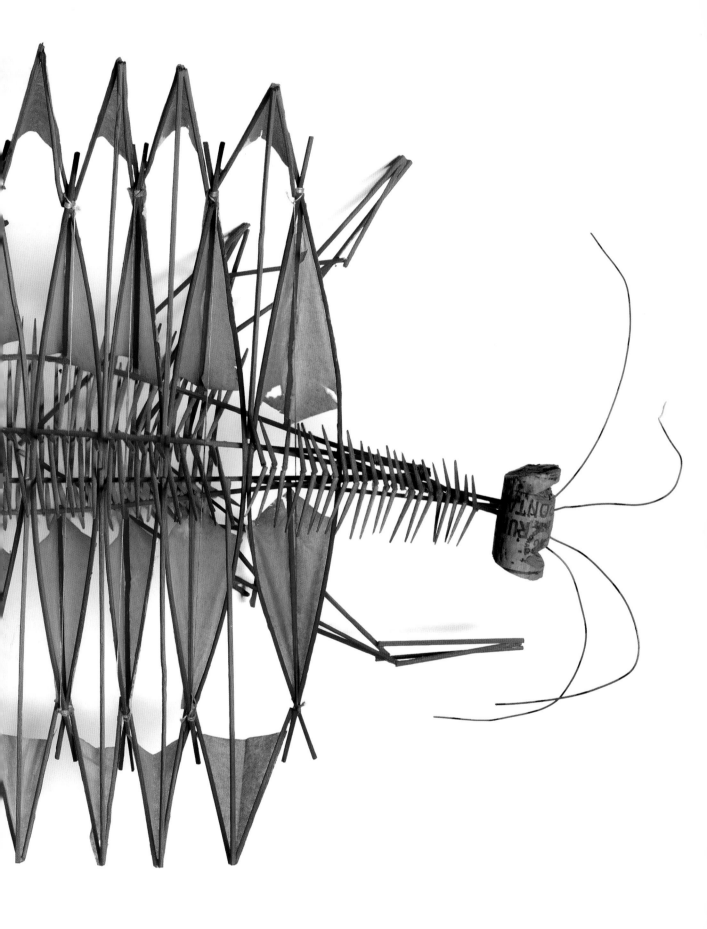

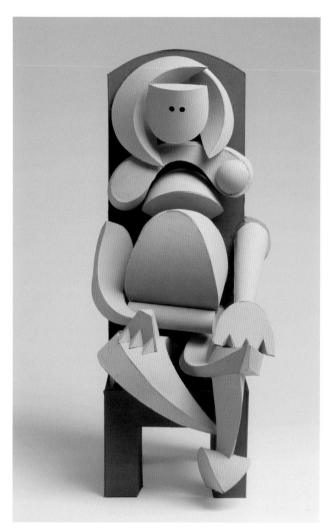

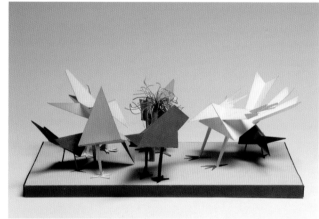

LEFT TO RIGHT:
PAINTED PAPERBOARD
6X8X19 INCHES

PAINTED CONSTRUCTION PAPER, TELEPHONE CABLE WIRE, WOOD DOWELS, NAILS
6.5X18.25X8.75 INCHES

BALSA WOOD, WOOD BASE
13.5 X 17 X 9 INCHES

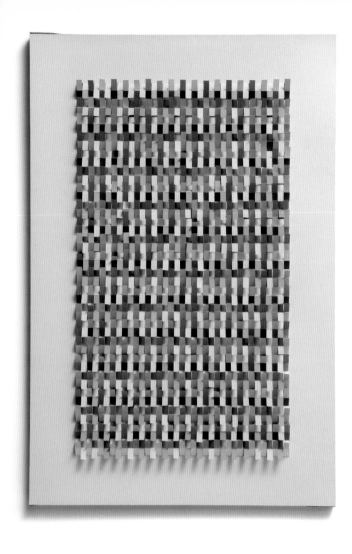

COLOR CONSTRUCTION PAPER, MAT-BOARD BASE
20.25 X 30 X 2.5 INCHES

COLOR CONSTRUCTION PAPER, WOOD BASE
7X7X19 INCHES

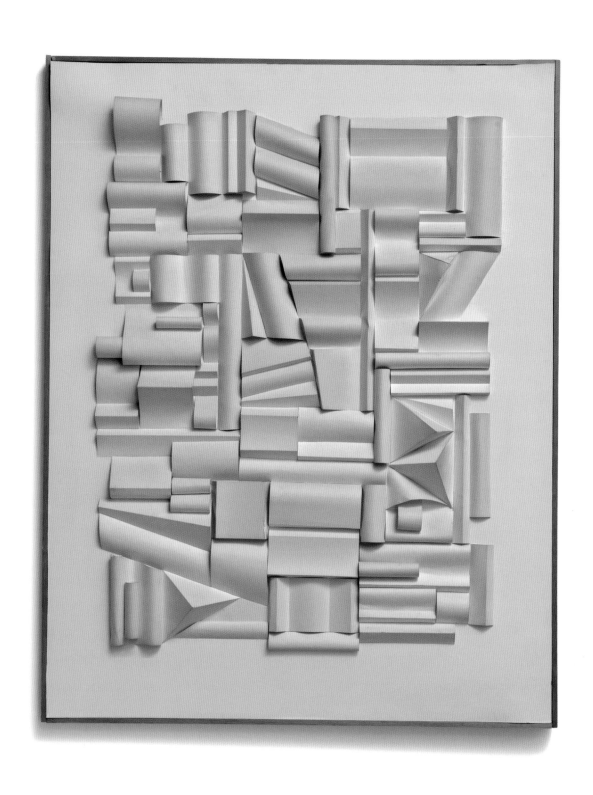

CONSTRUCTION PAPER, MAT-BOARD, WOOD FRAME
23X29X2.5 INCHES

MAT-BOARD, COLOR CONSTRUCTION PAPER, WOOD BASE
16.5 X 20.5 X 2 INCHES

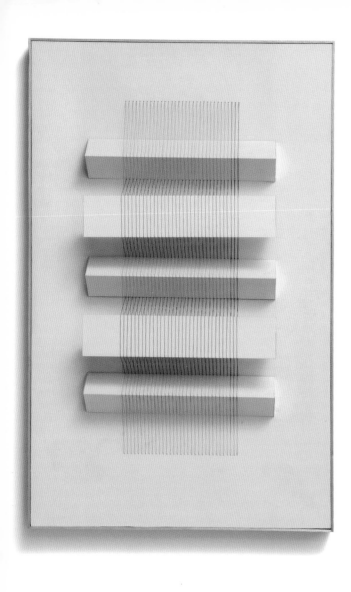

MAT-BOARD, CONSTRUCTION PAPER, COTTON THREADS, WOOD BASE
16.75 X 25.5 X 4.5 INCHES

PREVIOUS SPREAD:
TOOTHPICKS, DOLL HEAD, PINECONES, FOUND PINE-WOOD BASE
9 X 16 X 8 INCHES

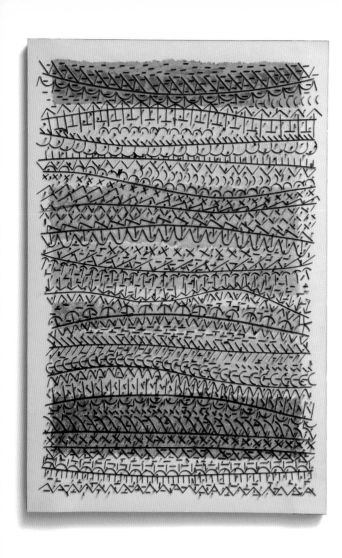

PAINTED WINDOW-BLIND MATCHSTICKS, MAT-BOARD, WOOD BASE
14.75 X 2 X 1.25 INCHES

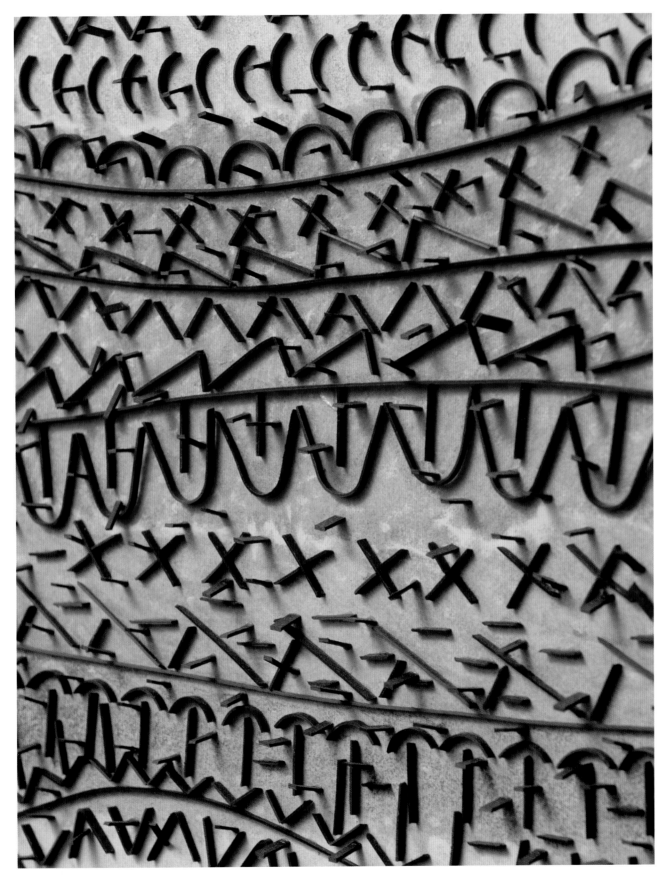

LEFT TO RIGHT:
PAINTED CONSTRUCTION BOARD
14X18X54 INCHES

CONSTRUCTION PAPER, MAT-BOARD, WOOD BASE
12X12X18 INCHES

PAPERBOARD, PAINTED PAPER, WOOD BOWL, ANTIQUE CANDLESTICK, WOOD BASE
25.5 X 18 X 10.25 INCHES

PLASTIC DOLL PARTS, GLASS DOLL EYES, MUFFIN TIN
7X10X5 INCHES

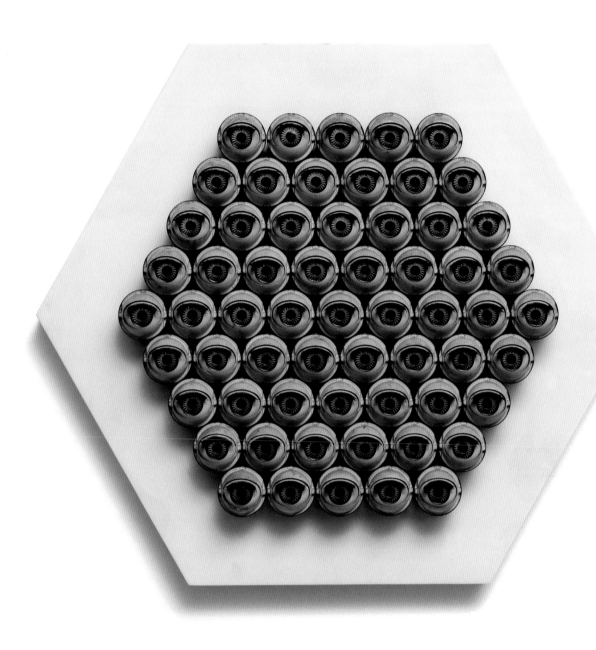

GLASS DOLL EYES, WOOD BASE
15X14X2.5 INCHES

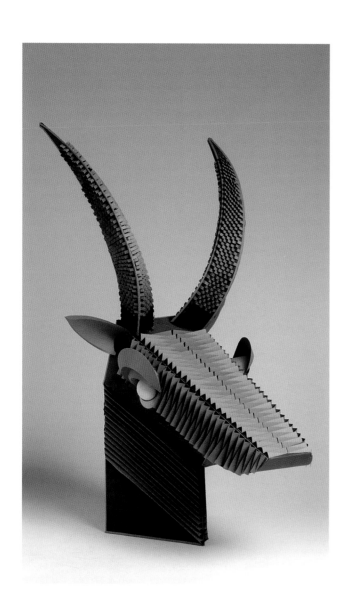

CONSTRUCTION PAPER, PING-PONG BALLS
12X15X25 INCHES

COLOR CONSTRUCTION PAPER, WOOD BASE
7X17X10 INCHES

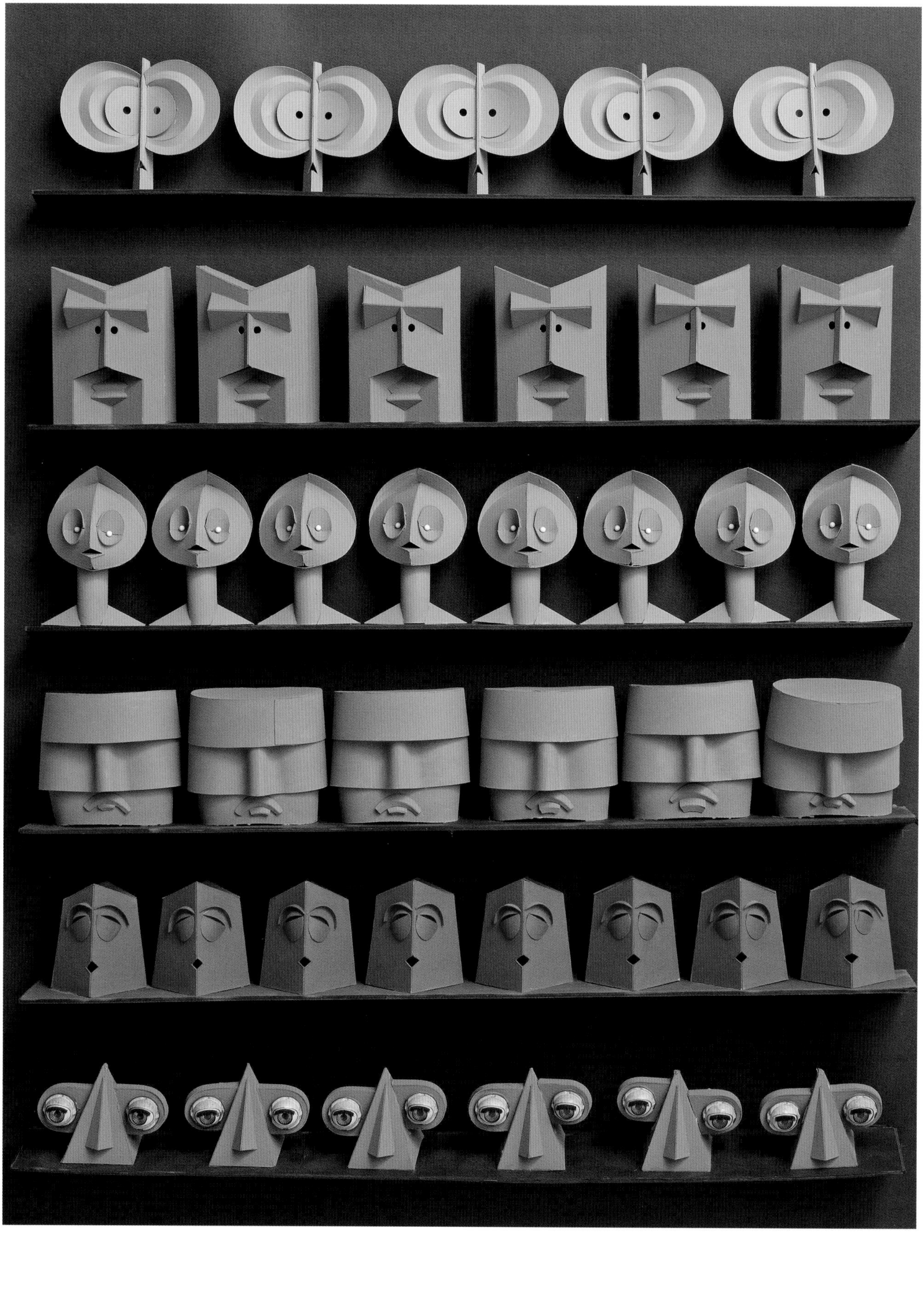

149

PREVIOUS SPREAD, LEFT TO RIGHT:
CONSTRUCTION PAPER, HAT PINS, GLASS DOLL EYES, MAT-BOARD BASE
32X40X5.75 INCHES

PAINTED CONSTRUCTION PAPER, MAT-BOARD BASE
32X40X4.5 INCHES

THIS PAGE:
LIGHT SOCKETS, 15-WATT LIGHT BULBS
19X3X16 INCHES

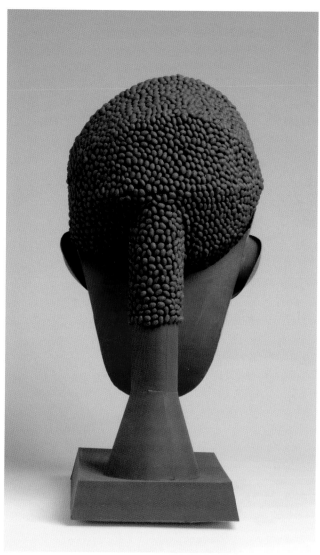

PAINTED PAPERBOARD, DRIED BEANS
8X10X17.5 INCHES

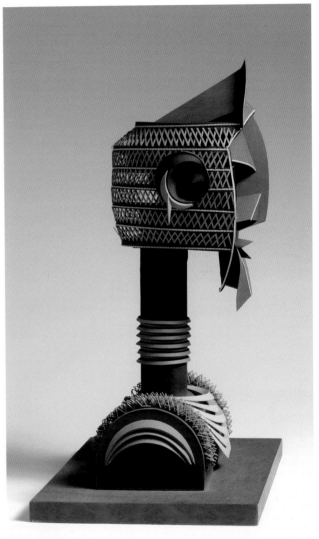

LEFT TO RIGHT:
CARDBOARD
9X11X31 INCHES

CONSTRUCTION PAPER, WOOD BASE
10X7X17 INCHES

CONSTRUCTION PAPER, GLASS EYES
24 X 11.5 X 18 INCHES

LEFT TO RIGHT:
CONSTRUCTION PAPER
8 X 24 X 14 INCHES

CONSTRUCTION PAPER
9.5 X 31 X 8 INCHES

PAINTED CONSTRUCTION PAPER
14 X 27 X 9 INCHES

CONSTRUCTION PAPER, CONSTRUCTION BOARD
13.25 X 24 X 10.75 INCHES

PAINTED PAPERBOARD
7 X 13.5 X 23 INCHES

PAINTED CONSTRUCTION PAPER, PAINTED WOOD BASE
40X30X4 INCHES

PAINTED PAPERBOARD
17X9X31 INCHES

CONSTRUCTION PAPER, TEMPERA PAINT
11X23X11 INCHES

162

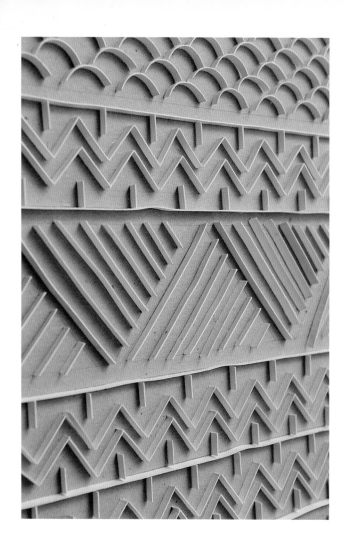

CONSTRUCTION PAPER, MAT-BOARD
22X28X2 INCHES

COLOR CONSTRUCTION PAPER, PAINTED MAT-BOARD, TWINE, WOOD DOWELS, WOOD BASE
24.25X32X8.25 INCHES

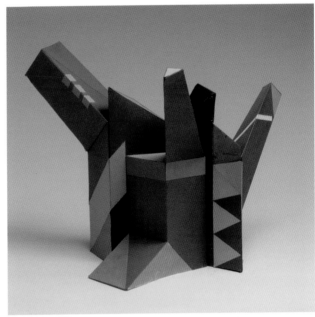

CLOCKWISE, LEFT TO RIGHT:
PAINTED CONSTRUCTION BOARD
18X18X19 INCHES

COLOR CONSTRUCTION PAPER
13X13X14.5 INCHES

COLOR CONSTRUCTION PAPER, PAINTED TOOTHPICKS, MAT-BOARD BASE
13X12X13 INCHES

VISITS WITH IRVING

USCHI WEISSMÜLLER

I first met Irving Harper in 2000 when I visited him at his home in Rye, New York. We had lunch together with his eighty-one-year-old wife, Belle, on their porch. Finding his house was almost impossible, hidden as it is in a neighborhood of winding tree-lined streets.

Working on this book, I've since visited Irving many times, but finding his hidden driveway is as difficult as ever. The feeling of being lost prevails until I see the name "Harper" hand-painted in black letters on a wood plank nailed to his barn. A dirt road leads to a colossal tree—a massive, ancient American beech at the center of a roundabout driveway—announcing that I've arrived. Irving says he and his wife bought the house because of it, and I think he finds his strength and longevity in it.

Every time I enter the world of Irving it is a surprise all over again. With each visit I am visually overwhelmed by the craftsmanship displayed on almost every surface of his three-story home. The living room is a "living" room in the truest sense. Irving spends most of his time here, reading in his chair and listening to classical music on his appropriately analog Walkman. It also holds the bulk of the work featured in this book.

In February 2010 we went to see Irving every day for a week to photograph this private collection of sculptures, this museum for one. Spending full days there, having lunch together, I was able to experience the cycles of light, finding new views and details. The house is full of vivid color, oranges and greens and yellows that have been there forever, so long that they feel new again.

On every visit I would ask Irving if there was anything I could bring him from the city. He always responded that he needed nothing, just another visit. One day I noticed that his pendulum clock was quiet—it had stopped working years ago, he said. It took three months for the clock to be repaired, but he was happy to have it returned to fill the blank space on the wall next to his fireplace. Two months later, the clock was still once again. Irving explained that he had grown used to the silence.

I took my parents to meet him recently. They were overwhelmed by his work and life. He asked my mother how old she was. When she told him, he responded, "Oh, to be seventy-three again!"

FIRST PUBLISHED IN THE UNITED STATES OF AMERICA IN 2013 BY
SKIRA RIZZOLI PUBLICATIONS, INC.
300 PARK AVENUE SOUTH
NEW YORK, NY 10010
WWW.RIZZOLIUSA.COM

ISBN-13: 978-0-8478-4001-4
LIBRARY OF CONGRESS CONTROL NUMBER: 201294281

PHOTOGRAPHY CREDITS
© D. James Dee: All sculpture photography

Courtesy Irving Harper Archive: 2-3, 6, 8, 10 center left, 10 center right, 10 bottom, 12 top, 16, 18, 19, 22, 23, 24 top right, 24 bottom, 28, 29 top, 29 bottom right, 30 center, 32, 33, 36 top, 36 bottom, 38 top

Courtesy Herman Miller Archive: 10 top left, 10 top right, 20, 29 bottom left, 36 center

© Leslie Williamson: Harper residence photography, except 30 bottom left and bottom center, 38 bottom, 108-109, 168 © D. James Dee

Courtesy Maharam: 30 top

© Vitra/Photography: Andreas Sütterlin (George Nelson Howard Miller Clocks): All images 26 and 27 except for 26 top left, 26 center right, 27 bottom center © Vitra/Photography: Marc Eggimann

Courtesy Vitra Design Museum Archive: 14, 15, 24 top left, 34 top, 37

with thanks to Yang Chung Punel

DESIGN AND PRODUCTION
A4 Studio: Allen Bianchi, Robert Ortega, Nicholas Savage, Uschi Weissmüller

Set in Calibre Light and Shift Book and Light Italic

EDITOR
Dung Ngo

Distributed to the U.S. Trade by Random House, New York

Printed in China

2013 2014 2015 2016 / 10 9 8 7 6 5 4 3

maharam